Barefoot Days
POEMS OF CHILDHOOD

This book belongs to

"**Poetry** is the record of the best
and happiest moments of the
happiest and best minds."
Percy Bysshe Shelley

Barefoot Days
POEMS OF CHILDHOOD

Poems Selected by Julie Shively
Illustrated by Russ Flint

An Imprint of Ideals Publications Incorporated
Nashville, Tennessee

Contents

THE WORLD AROUND US --- 8

    Feet --- 9

    The World --- 10

    Sea Shell --- 11

    My Land Is Fair for Any Eyes to See ------------------- 13

    A Violet Bank -- 13

    Be Different to Trees --------------------------------- 13

    Water --- 14

    Spring Rain -- 14

    One Misty, Moisty Morning --------------------------- 14

    Doctor Foster -- 14

    In Time of Silver Rain -------------------------------- 14

    April Rain --- 15

    What Do We Plant? ----------------------------------- 16

    To the Wayfarer -------------------------------------- 16

    Snowflakes -- 18

    The Wind -- 19

    Who Has Seen the Wind? ----------------------------- 19

    Velvet Shoes --- 19

READING, DREAMS, AND IMAGINATION -------------------------- 20

    Knight-in-Armour ----------------------------------- 20

    I Wouldn't Be Afraid -------------------------------- 20

    A Book -- 20

    Dreams --- 22

    When Mother Reads Aloud --------------------------- 23

    Be Like the Bird ------------------------------------- 23

    It Is Raining -- 24

    Hold Fast Your Dreams ------------------------------- 26

    To Dark Eyes Dreaming ------------------------------ 26

    The Little Green Orchard ----------------------------- 29

    The Library -- 30

    I'd Leave -- 31

    Who Hath a Book ------------------------------------ 32

    I've Got a New Book from Grandfather Hyde ----------- 33

    Mr. Nobody --- 33

    The Land of Story-Books ----------------------------- 33

HOME AND MANNERS -- 34

    Of Courtesy --- 35

    Whole Duty of Children ------------------------------ 35

Politeness -------- 35
Learning -------- 35
Good Night -------- 36
Evening Hymn -------- 36
Good Night -------- 36
In the Garden -------- 38
House Blessing -------- 39
My Garden -------- 39
Little Things -------- 39
Winter Night -------- 40
I Never Hear -------- 41
Only One Mother -------- 41
Cradle Song -------- 41
Animal Crackers -------- 42
Evening Song -------- 42
Morning Song -------- 42
The Moon -------- 44
The Moon -------- 44

FUN AND PLAY -------- 46
Good and Bad Children -------- 46
The Swing -------- 47
Puddles -------- 49
April Rain Song -------- 49
Beauty -------- 49
Afternoon on a Hill -------- 50
Childhood -------- 50
Swift Things Are Beautiful -------- 51
Come, Little Leaves -------- 52
The Sun -------- 53
Laughing Song -------- 53
Frolic -------- 54
My Shadow -------- 54
We Thank Thee -------- 56
Fun in a Garret -------- 57
A Good Play -------- 57
Lesson from a Sun-Dial -------- 57

GOOD FRIENDS AND LOYAL PALS -------- 58
Doorbells -------- 58
Crocuses -------- 58
The Snowman -------- 60
Three Things to Remember -------- 61
Hurt No Living Thing -------- 61

A Bird Came Down the Walk --- 62

Little Robin Redbreast -- 62

Caterpillar --- 62

Friends -- 65

There Isn't Time --- 65

Kindness to Animals -- 66

Hearth --- 66

Donkey, Donkey -- 66

Poem -- 66

This Happy Day --- 67

The Secret --- 68

What Robin Told -- 68

The Little Busy Bee --- 68

HOLIDAYS AND HAPPY DAYS -- 70

Summer Vacation --- 71

Sprinkling -- 71

The Star-Spangled Banner --- 72

The Flag Goes By --- 72

I Hear America Singing -- 73

Theme in Yellow -- 75

Hallowe'en --- 75

The First Thanksgiving of All -- 76

The Pilgrim --- 76

The Pilgrims Came -- 77

We Thank Thee --- 77

The Christmas Silence -- 78

A Christmas Folk Song -- 79

Jesus, Our Brother --- 81

Long, Long Ago -- 82

The Shepherd and the King --- 83

Christmas Carol -- 83

My Gift -- 84

Bells of Christmas -- 84

INDEX OF AUTHORS -- 86

INDEX OF TITLES -- 87

ACKNOWLEDGMENTS (continued) --------------------------------- 88

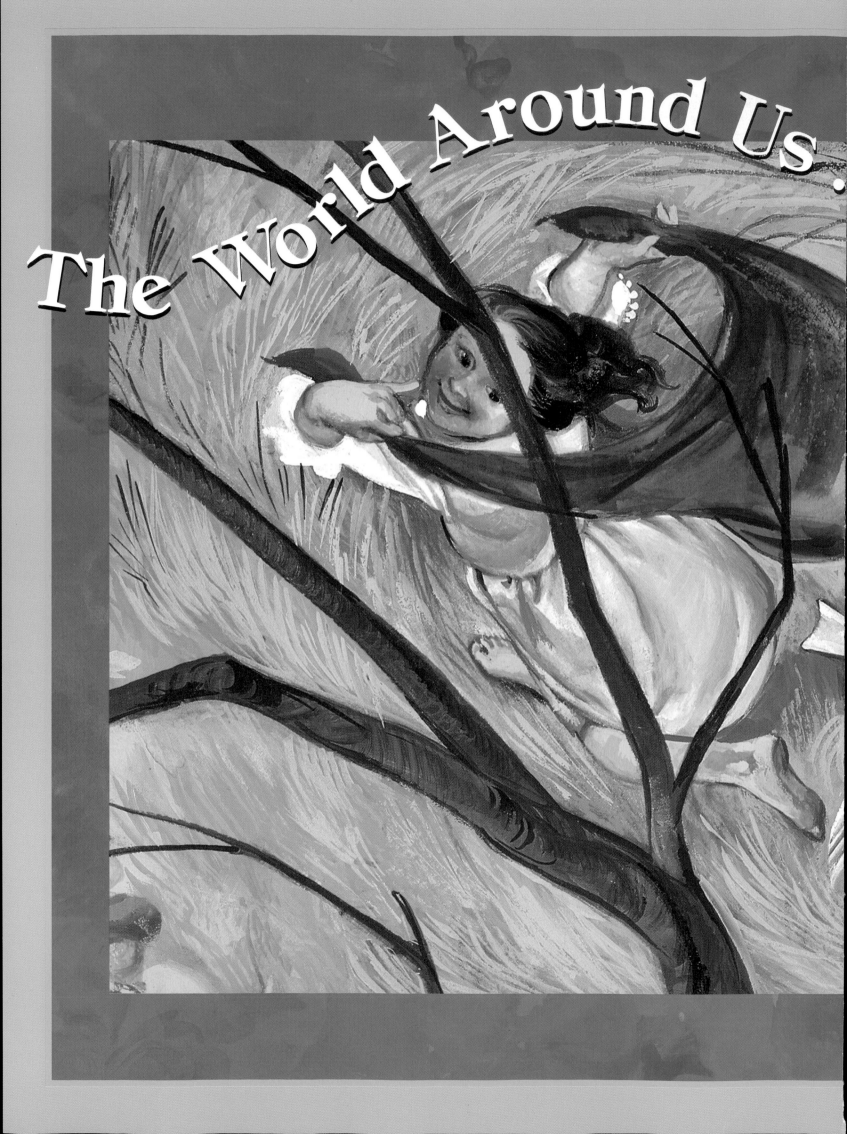

The World Around Us

FEET

There are things feet know
That hands never will:
The exciting pounding feel
Of running down a hill;

The soft cool prickliness
When feet are bare
Walking in the summer grass
To most anywhere;

Or dabbling in water all
Slip-sliddering through toes—
(Nicer than through fingers, though *why*
No one really knows.)

"Toes, tell my fingers," I
Said to them one day,
"Why it's such fun just to
Wiggle and play."

But toes just looked at me
Solemn and still.
Oh, there are things feet know
That hands never will.

Dorothy Aldis

THE WORLD

Great, wide, beautiful, wonderful World,
With the wonderful water round you curled,
And the wonderful grass upon your breast,
World, you are beautifully drest.

The wonderful air is over me,
And the wonderful wind is shaking the tree,
It walks on the water and whirls the mills,
And talks to itself on the tops of the hills.

You friendly Earth! how far do you go,
With the wheat-fields that nod and the rivers that flow,
With cities and gardens and cliffs and isles,
And people upon you for thousands of miles?

Ah! you are so great, and I am so small,
I tremble to think of you, World, at all;
And yet, when I said my prayers today,
A whisper inside me seemed to say,
"You are more than the Earth, though you are such a dot:
You can love and think, and the Earth cannot!"

William Brighty Rands

SEA SHELL

Sea Shell, Sea Shell,
Sing me a song, O please!

A song of ships, and sailormen,
And parrots, and tropical trees,
Of islands lost in the Spanish Main
Which no man ever may find again,
Of fishes and corals under the waves,
And sea horses stabled in great green caves.

Sea Shell, Sea Shell,
Sing of the things you know so well.

Amy Lowell

MY LAND IS FAIR
FOR ANY EYES TO SEE

My land is fair for any eyes to see—
No look, my friends—look to the east and west!
You see the purple hills far in the west—
Hills lined with pine and gum and black-oak tree—
Now to the east you see the fertile valley!
This land is mine, I sing of it to you—
My land is mine, I sing of it to you—
My land beneath the skies of white and blue.
This land is mine, for I am part of it.
I am the land, for it is part of me—
We are akin and thus our kinship be!
It would make me a brother to the tree!
And far as eyes can see this land is mine.
Not for one foot of it I have a deed—
To own this land I do not need a deed—
They all belong to me—gum, oak, and pine.

Jesse Stuart

A VIOLET BANK

I know a bank whereon the
        wild thyme blows,
Where oxlips and the nodding
        violet grows:
Quite over-canopied with
        lush woodbine,
With sweet musk roses and with
        eglantine.

William Shakespeare

BE DIFFERENT
TO TREES

The talking oak
To the ancients spoke.
But any tree
Will talk to me.

What truths I know
I garnered so.

But those who want to talk and tell,
And those who will not listeners be,
Will never hear a syllable
From out the lips of any tree.

Mary Carolyn Davies

SPRING RAIN

Leaves make a slow
Whispering sound
As down the drops go
Drip to the ground
       Peace, peace, says the tree.

Good wet rain!
Shout happy frogs,
Peepers and big green
Bulls in bogs,
       Lucky, lucky are we!

Harry Behn

DOCTOR FOSTER

Doctor Foster went to Gloucester
In a shower of rain;
He stepped in a puddle, up to his middle,
And never went there again.

Author Unknown

WATER

The world turns softly
Not to spill its lakes and rivers.
The water is held in its arms
And the sky is held in the water.
What is water,
That pours silver,
And can hold the sky?

Hilda Conkling

IN TIME OF SILVER RAIN

In time of silver rain
The earth
Puts forth new life again,
Green grasses grow
And flowers lift their heads,
And over all the plain
The wonder spreads
       Of life,
       Of life,
       Of life!

In time of silver rain
The butterflies
Lift silken wings
To catch a rainbow cry,
And trees put forth
New leaves to sing
In joy beneath the sky
As down the roadway
Passing boys and girls
Go singing, too,
In time of silver rain
       When spring
       And life
       Are new.

Langston Hughes

ONE MISTY, MOISTY MORNING

One misty, moisty morning,
When cloudy was the weather,
I chanced to meet an old man
Clothed all in leather.
He began to compliment,
And I began to grin,
How do you do, and how do you do,
And how do you do again?

Author Unknown

14

APRIL RAIN

It is not raining rain to me,
　It's raining daffodils;
In every dimpled drop I see
　Wild flowers on the hills.
The clouds of gray engulf the day
　And overwhelm the town;
It is not raining rain to me,
　It's raining roses down.

It is not raining rain to me,
　But fields of clover bloom
Where every buccaneering bee
　May find a bed and room.
A health unto the happy!
　A fig for him who frets!
It is not raining rain to me,
　It's raining violets.

Robert Loveman

15

What Do We Plant?

What do we plant when we plant the tree?
We plant the ship, which will cross the sea.
We plant the mast to carry the sails;
We plant the planks to withstand the gales—
The keel, the keelson, the beam, the knee;
We plant the ship when we plant the tree.

What do we plant when we plant the tree?
We plant the houses for you and me.
We plant the rafters, the shingles, the floors,
We plant the studding, the lath, the doors,
The beams and siding, all parts that be;
We plant the house when we plant the tree.

What do we plant when we plant the tree?
A thousand things that we daily see;
We plant the spire that out-towers the crag,
We plant the staff for our country's flag,
We plant the shade, from the hot sun free;
We plant all these when we plant the tree.

Henry Abbey

To the Wayfarer

A Poem Fastened to Trees in the Portuguese Forests

Ye who pass by and would raise your hand against
me, hearken ere you harm me.

I am the heat of your hearth on the cold winter nights,
the friendly shade screening you from summer sun, and
my fruits are refreshing draughts, quenching your
thirst as you journey on.

I am the beam that holds your house, the board of your table,
the bed on which you lie, the timber that builds your boat.

I am the handle of your hoe, the door of your homestead, the wood of
your cradle, and the shell of your coffin.

I am the bread of kindness and the flower of beauty.
Ye who pass by, listen to my prayer: harm me not.

Author Unknown

SNOWFLAKES

Whenever a snowflake leaves the sky,
It turns and turns to say, "Goodbye!
Goodbye, dear clouds, so cool and gray!"
Then lightly travels on its way.

And when a snowflake finds a tree,
"Good day!" it says, "Good day to thee!
Thou art so bare and lonely, dear,
I'll rest and call my comrades here."

But when a snowflake, brave and meek,
Lights on a rosy maiden's cheek,
It starts, "How warm and soft the day!
'Tis summer!" and it melts away.

Mary Mapes Dodge

THE WIND

I saw you toss the kites on high
And blow the birds about the sky;
And all around I heard you pass,
Like ladies' skirts across the grass—

O wind, a-blowing all day long,
O wind that sings so loud a song!

I saw the different things you did,
But always you yourself you hid.
I felt you push, I heard you call,
I could not see yourself at all—

O wind, a-blowing all day long,
O wind that sings so loud a song!

O you that are so strong and cold,
O blower, are you young or old?
Are you a beast of field and tree,
Or just a stronger child than me?

O wind, a-blowing all day long,
O wind that sings so loud a song!

Robert Louis Stevenson

WHO HAS SEEN THE WIND?

Who has seen the wind?
Neither I nor you:
But when the leaves
hang trembling
The wind is passing
through.

Who has seen the wind?
Neither you nor I:
But when the trees
bow down their heads,
The wind is passing by.

Christina Rossetti

VELVET SHOES

Let us walk in the white snow
In a soundless space;
With footsteps quiet and slow,
At a tranquil pace,
Under veils of white lace.

I shall go shod in silk,
And you in wool,
White as a white cow's milk,
More beautiful
Than the breast of a gull.

We shall walk through the still town
In a windless peace;
We shall step upon white down,
Upon silver fleece,
Upon softer than these.

We shall walk in velvet shoes:
Wherever we go
Silence will fall like dews
On white silence below.
We shall walk in the snow.

Elinor Wylie

Reading, Dreams, and

KNIGHT-IN-ARMOUR

Whenever I'm a shining Knight,
I buckle on my armour tight;
And then I look about for things,
Like Rushings-Out, and Rescuings,
And Savings from the Dragon's Lair,
And fighting all the Dragons there.
And sometimes when our fights begin,
I think I'll let the Dragons win . . .
And then I think perhaps I won't,
Because they're Dragons, and I don't.

A. A. Milne

I WOULDN'T BE AFRAID

I wouldn't be afraid to fight a demon or a dragon, if you'd dare me.
I wouldn't be afraid of witches, warlocks, trolls, or giants.
Just worms scare me.

Judith Viorst

A BOOK

There is no Frigate like a Book
To take us Lands away,
Nor any Coursers like a Page
Of prancing Poetry—
This Traverse may the poorest take
Without oppress of Toll—
How frugal is the Chariot
That bears a Human soul.

Emily Dickinson

Imagination . . . .

DREAMS

Hold fast to dreams
For if dreams die
Life is a broken-winged bird
That cannot fly.

Hold fast to dreams
For when dreams go
Life is a barren field
Frozen with snow.

Langston Hughes

WHEN MOTHER READS ALOUD

When Mother reads aloud, the past
Seems real as every day;
I hear the tramp of armies vast,
I see the spears and lances cast,
I join the trilling fray;
Brave knights and ladies fair and proud
I meet when Mother reads aloud.

When Mother reads aloud, far lands
Seem very near and true;
I cross the desert's gleaming sands,
Or hunt the jungle's prowling bands,
Or sail the ocean blue.
Far heights, whose peaks the cold mists shroud,
I scale when Mother reads aloud.

When Mother reads aloud, I long
For noble deeds to do.
To help the right, redress the wrong;
It seems so easy to be strong,
So simple to be true.
Oh, thick and fast the visions crowd
My eyes, when Mother reads aloud.

Author Unknown

BE LIKE THE BIRD

Be like the bird, who
Halting in his flight
On limb too slight
Feels it give way beneath him,
Yet sings
Knowing he hath wings.

Victor Hugo

IT IS RAINING

It is raining.

Where would you like to be in the rain?
Where would you like to be?

I'd like to be on a city street,
where the rain comes down in a driving sheet,
where it wets the houses—roof and wall—
the wagons and horses and autos and all.
That's where I'd like to be in the rain,
that's where I'd like to be.

It is raining.

Where would you like to be in the rain?
Where would you like to be?

I'd like to be in a tall tree top,
where the rain comes dripping, drop, drop, drop,
around on every side:
where it wets the farmer, the barn, the pig,
the cows, the chickens both little and big;
where it batters and beats on a field of wheat
and makes the little birds hide.

It is raining.

Where would you like to be in the rain?
Where would you like to be?

I'd like to be on a ship at sea,
where everything's wet as wet can be
and the waves are rolling high,
where sailors are pulling the ropes and singing,
and wind's in the rigging and salt spray's stinging,
and round us sea gulls cry.
On a dripping skimming ship at sea—
that's where I'd like to be in the rain;
that's where I'd like to be!

Lucy Sprague Mitchell

HOLD FAST YOUR DREAMS

Within your heart
Keep one still, secret spot
Where dreams may go,
And sheltered so,
May thrive and grow—
Where doubt and fear are not.
Oh, keep a place apart
Within your heart,
For little dreams to go.

Louise Driscoll

TO DARK EYES DREAMING

Dreams go fast and far these days.
They go by rocket thrust.
They go arrayed
    in lights
        or in the dust of stars.
Dreams, these days,
    go fast and far.
Dreams are young, these days,
    or very old,
They can be black
    or blue or gold.
They need no special charts,
    nor any fuel.
It seems, only one rule applies,
    to all our dreams—
They will not fly except in open sky.
    A fenced-in dream
        will die.

Zilpha Keatley Snyder

THE LITTLE GREEN ORCHARD

Someone is always sitting there,
      In the little green orchard;
   Even when the sun in high,
   In noon's unclouded sky,
   And faintly droning goes
   The bee from rose to rose,
Someone in shadow is sitting there,
      In the little green orchard.

Yes, and when twilight's falling softly
      On the little green orchard;
   When the grey dew distills
   And every flower-cup fills;
   When the last blackbird says,
   "What—what!" and goes her way—ssh!
I have heard voices calling softly
      In the little green orchard.

Not that I am afraid of being there,
      In the little green orchard;
   Why, when the moon's been bright,
   Shedding her lonesome light,
   And moths like ghosties come,
   And the horned snail leaves home:
I've sat there, whispering and listening there,
      In the little green orchard.

Only it's strange to be feeling there,
      In the little green orchard;
   Whether you paint or draw,
   Dig, hammer, chop, or saw;
   When you are most alone.
   All but the silence gone . . .
Someone is waiting and watching there,
      In the little green orchard.

Walter de la Mare

THE LIBRARY

It looks like any building
When you pass it on the street,
Made of stone and glass and marble,
Made of iron and concrete.

But once inside you can ride
A camel or a train,
Visit Rome, Siam, or Nome,
Feel a hurricane,
Meet a king, learn to sing,
How to bake a pie,
Go to sea, plant a tree,
Find how airplanes fly,
Train a horse, and, of course,
Have all the dogs you'd like,
See the moon, a sandy dune,
Or catch a whopping pike.

Everything that books can bring
You'll find inside those walls.
A world is there for you to share
When adventure calls.

You cannot tell its magic
By the way the building looks,
But there's wonderment within it—
The wonderment of books.

Barbara A. Huff

I'd Leave

I'd leave all the hurry,
the noise and the fray
For a house full of books
and a garden of flowers.

Andrew Lang

WHO HATH A BOOK

Who hath a **book**
Hath friends at hand,
And gold and gear
At his command;
And rich estates,
 If he but look,
 Are held by him
Who hath a **book**.

Who hath a **book**
Hath but to read
And he may be
A king, indeed.
His kingdom is
His inglenook—
All this is his
Who hath a **book**.

Wilbur D. Nesbit

I've Got a New Book from My Grandfather Hyde

I've got a new book from my Grandfather Hyde.
It's skin on the cover and paper inside,
And reads about Arabs and horses and slaves,
And tells how the Caliph of Bagdad behaves.
I'd not take a goat and a dollar beside
For the book that I got from my Grandfather Hyde.

Leroy F. Jackson

The Land of Story-Books

At evening when the lamp is lit,
Around the fire my parents sit;
They sit at home and talk and sing,
And do not play at anything.

Now, with my little gun, I crawl
All in the dark along the wall,
And follow round the forest track
Away behind the sofa back.

There, in the night, where none can spy,
All in my hunter's camp I lie,
And play at books that I have read
Till it is time to go to bed.

These are the hills, these are the woods,
These are my starry solitudes;
And there the river by whose brink
The roaring lions come to drink.

I see the others far away
As if in firelit camp they lay,
And I, like to an Indian scout,
Around their party prowled about.

So, when my nurse comes in for me,
Home I return across the sea,
And go to bed with backward looks
At my dear Land of Story-Books.

Robert Louis Stevenson

Mr. Nobody

I know a funny little man,
As quiet as a mouse,
Who does the mischief that is done
In everybody's house!
There's no one ever sees his face,
And yet we all agree
That every plate we break was cracked
By Mr. Nobody.

'Tis he who always tears our books,
Who leaves the door ajar;
He pulls the buttons from our shirts,
And scatters pins afar;
That squeaking door will always squeak,
For, prithee, don't you see,
We leave the oiling to be done
By Mr. Nobody.

The finger marks upon the door
By none of us are made;
We never leave the blinds unclosed,
To let the curtains fade.
The ink we never spill; the boots
That lying round you see
Are not our boots—they all belong
To Mr. Nobody.

Author Unknown

Home
and Manners . . . .

OF COURTESY

Good Manners may in Seven Words be found:
Forget Yourself and think of Those Around.

Arthur Guiterman

WHOLE DUTY OF CHILDREN

A child should always say what's true
And speak when he is spoken to,
And behave mannerly at table:
At least as far as he is able.

Robert Louis Stevenson

POLITENESS

If people ask me,
I always tell them:
"Quite well, thank you, I'm
     very glad to say."
If people ask me,
I always answer,
"Quite well, thank you, how are
     you today?"
I always answer,
I always tell them,
If they ask me
Politely. . . .
BUT SOMETIMES
               I wish
          That they wouldn't.

A. A. Milne

LEARNING

I'm learning to say thank you.
And I'm learning to say please.
And I'm learning to use Kleenex,
Not my sweater, when I sneeze.
And I'm learning not to dribble.
And I'm learning not to slurp.
And I'm learning (though it some-
     times really hurts me)
Not to burp.
And I'm learning to chew softer
When I eat corn on the cob.
And I'm learning that it's much
Much easier to be a slob.

Judith Viorst

GOOD NIGHT

On tip-toe comes the gentle dark
To help the children sleep,
And silently, in silver paths,
The slumber fairies creep.

Then overhead, God sees that all
His candles are a-light,
And reaching loving arms to us,
He bids His world Good Night.

Dorothy Mason Pierce

EVENING HYMN

Gentle Jesus, meek and mild,
Look upon a little child.
Make me gentle as Thou art,
Come and live within my heart.
Take my childish hand in Thine,
Guide these little feet of mine.
So shall all my happy days
Sing their pleasant song of praise;
And the world shall always see
Christ, the Holy Child, in me.

Charles Wesley

GOOD NIGHT

Good night! good night!
Far flies the light;
But still God's love
Shall flame above,
Making all bright.
Good night! good night!

Victor Hugo

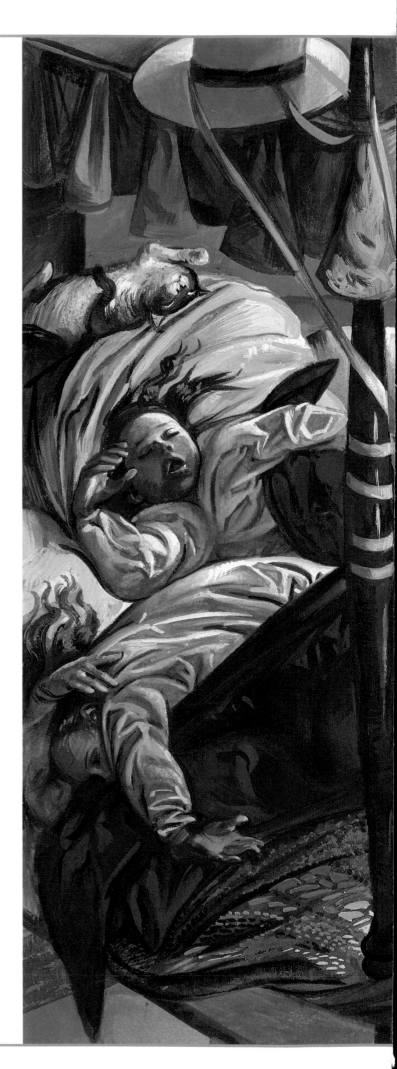

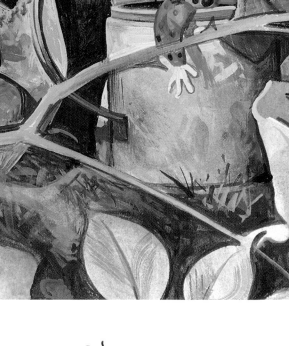

IN THE GARDEN

I spied beside the garden bed
A tiny lass of ours
Who stopped and bent her sunny head
Above the red June flowers.

Pushing the leaves and thorns apart,
She singled out a rose
And in its inmost crimson heart,
Enraptured, plunged her nose.

"O dear, dear rose, come, tell me true,
Come, tell me true," said she,
"If I smell just as sweet to you
As you smell sweet to me!"

Ernest Crosby

HOUSE BLESSING

Bless the four corners of this house,
And be the lintel blest;
And bless the heart and bless the board
And bless each place of rest;
And bless the door that opens wide
To stranger as to kin;
And bless each crystal window-pane
That lets the starlight in;
And bless the rooftree overhead
And every sturdy wall.
The peace of man, the peace of God,
The peace of Love on all!

Arthur Guiterman

MY GARDEN

A garden is a lovesome thing, God wot!
    Rose plot,
    Fringed pool
Fern'd grot—
    The veriest school
    Of peace; and yet the fool
Contends that God is not—
Not God! in gardens! when the eve is cool?
    Nay, but I have a sign;
    'Tis very sure God walks in mine.

Thomas Edward Brown

LITTLE THINGS

Little drops of water,
Little grains of sand,
Make the mighty ocean
And the pleasant land.

Thus the little minutes,
Humble though they be,
Make the mighty ages
Of eternity.

Thus our little errors
Lead the soul away

From the path of virtue,
Far in sin to stray.

Little deeds of kindness,
Little words of love,
Make our earth an Eden,
Like the heaven above.

Little seeds of mercy,
Sown by youthful hands,
Grow to bless the nations
In distant foreign lands.

Julia Fletcher Carney

WINTER NIGHT

Blow, wind, blow!
Drift the flying snow!
Send it twirling, whirling overhead!
There's a bedroom in a tree
Where, snug as snug can be,
The squirrel nests in his cozy bed.

Shriek, wind, shriek!
Make the branches creak!
Battle with the boughs till break o' day!
In a snow-cave warm and tight,
Through the icy winter night,
The rabbit sleeps the peaceful hours away.

Call, wind, call!
In entry and in hall!
Straight from off the mountain white and wild!
Soft purrs the pussy-cat
On her little fluffy mat,
And beside her nestles close her furry child.

Scold, wind, scold!
So bitter and so bold!
Shake the windows with your tap, tap, tap!
With half-shut, dreamy eyes,
The drowsy baby lies
Cuddled closely in his mother's lap.

Mary F. Butts

I NEVER HEAR

I never hear my mother come
Into my room late, late at night.
She says she has to look and see
If I'm still tucked exactly right.
Nor do I feel her kissing me.
She says she does, though,
Every night.

Dorothy Aldis

ONLY ONE MOTHER

Hundreds of stars in the pretty sky,
Hundreds of shells on the shore together,
Hundreds of birds that go singing by,
Hundreds of lambs in the sunny weather.

Hundreds of dewdrops to greet the dawn,
Hundreds of bees in the purple clover,
Hundreds of butterflies on the lawn,
But only one mother the wide world over.

George Cooper

CRADLE SONG

Sleep, baby, sleep,
Our cottage vale is deep;
The little lamb is on the green,
With wooly fleece so soft and clean,
Sleep, baby, sleep!

Sleep, baby, sleep,
Down where the woodbines creep;
Be always like the lamb so mild,
A kind and sweet and gentle child,
Sleep, baby, sleep!

Author Unknown

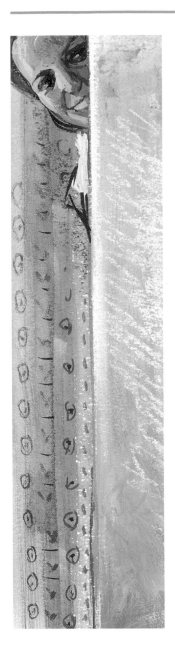

ANIMAL CRACKERS

Animal crackers, and cocoa to drink,
That is the finest of suppers, I think;
When I am grown up and can have what I please
I think I shall always insist upon these.

What do *you* choose when you're offered a treat?
When Mother says, "What would you like best to eat?"
Is it waffles and syrup, or cinnamon toast?
It's cocoa and animals that *I* love the most!

The kitchen's the cosiest place that I know:
The kettle is singing, the stove is aglow,
And there in the twilight, how jolly to see
The cocoa and animals waiting for me.

Daddy and Mother dine later in state,
With Mary to cook for them, Susan to wait;
But they don't have nearly as much fun as I
Who eat in the kitchen with Nurse standing by;
And Daddy once said he would like to be me
Having **cocoa** and **animals** once more for tea!

Christopher Morley

EVENING SONG

I hear no voice, I feel no touch,
I see no glory bright;
But yet I know that God is near
In darkness as in light.

He watches ever by my side,
And hears my whispered prayer,
That Father for His little child
Both day and night shall care.

Author Unknown

MORNING SONG

Father, we thank Thee for the night
And for the pleasant morning light,
For rest and food and loving care
And all that makes our life so fair.

Help us to do the things we should,
To be to others kind and good;
In all we do and all we say
To grow more loving every day.

Rebecca J. Weston

THE MOON

O look at the **moon**!
    She is shining up there;
O Mother, she looks
    like a lamp in the air.
Last week she was smaller
    and shaped like a bow;
But now she's grown bigger
    and round as an O.

Pretty **Moon**, pretty **Moon**,
    how you shine on the door
And make it all bright
    on my nursery floor!
You shine on my playthings
    and show me their place,
And I love to look up
    at your bright pretty face.

Eliza Lee Follen

THE MOON

The moon has a face like the clock in the hall;
She shines on thieves on the garden wall,
On streets and fields and harbor quays,
And birdies asleep in the forks of the trees.

The squalling cat and the squeaking mouse,
The howling dog by the door of the house,
The bat that lies in bed at noon,
All love to be out by the light of the moon.

But all of the things that belong to the day
Cuddle to sleep to be out of her way;
And flowers and children close their eyes
Till up in the morning the sun shall arise.

Robert Louis Stevenson

GOOD AND BAD CHILDREN

Children, you are very little,
And your bones are very brittle;
If you would grow great and stately,
You must try to walk sedately.

You must still be bright and quiet,
And content with simple diet;
And remain, through all bewild'ring,
Innocent and honest children.

Happy hearts and happy faces,
Happy play in grassy places—
That was how, in ancient ages,
Children grew to kings and sages.

Robert Louis Stevenson

THE SWING

How do you like to go up in a swing,
Up in the air so blue?
Oh, I do think it the pleasantest thing
Ever a child can do!

Up in the air and over the wall,
Till I can see so wide,
Rivers and trees and cattle and all
Over the countryside,

Till I look down on the garden green,
Down on the roof so brown—
Up in the air I go flying again,
Up in the air and down!

Robert Louis Stevenson

PUDDLES

I like to look in puddles—
When I smile,
they smile,
when I laugh,
they laugh,
and when I cry,
they don't mind getting wet.

Frank Asch

APRIL RAIN SONG

Let the rain kiss you.
Let the rain beat upon your head with silver liquid drops.
Let the rain sing you a lullaby.

The rain makes still pools on the sidewalk.
The rain makes running pools in the gutter.
The rain plays a little sleep-song on our roof at night—

And I love the rain.

Langston Hughes

BEAUTY

Beauty is seen
In the sunlight,
The trees, the birds,
Corn growing and people working
Or dancing for their harvest.

Beauty is heard
In the night,
Wind sighing, rain falling,
Or a singer chanting
Anything in earnest.

Beauty is in yourself.
Good deeds, happy thoughts
That repeat themselves
In your dreams,
In your work,
And even in your rest.

E-Yeh-Shure

49

AFTERNOON ON A HILL

I will be the gladdest thing
Under the sun!
I will touch a hundred flowers
And not pick one.

I will look at cliffs and clouds
With quiet eyes,
Watch the wind bow down the grass,
And the grass rise.

And when the lights begin to show
Up from the town,
I will mark which must be mine,
And then start down!

Edna St. Vincent Millay

CHILDHOOD

When birdsongs and hens fill the barnyard air
And from byre there comes the lowing,
When mist on the hills is rising fair,
All the little feet are going.

The game of tag and the bare pony ride,
The boat on the water gleaming,
The peat fire of evening and tale beside
Fill daytime till bedtime dreaming.

O God bless the girl and God bless the boy;
No ragwort-whip may they merit,
And as they grow, be they filled with Thy joy;
Thy kingdom may they inherit.

Author Unknown

SWIFT THINGS ARE BEAUTIFUL

Swift things are beautiful:
Swallows and deer,
And lightning that falls
Bright-veined and clear,
Rivers and meteors,
Wind in the wheat,
The strong-withered horse,
The runner's sure feet.

And slow things are beautiful:
The closing of day,
The pause of the wave
That curves downward to spray,
The ember that crumbles,
The opening flower,
And the ox that moves on
In the quiet of power.

Elizabeth Coatsworth

COME, LITTLE LEAVES

"Come, little leaves," said the wind one day,
"Come o'er the meadows with me and play;
Put on your dresses of red and gold,
For summer is gone and the days grow cold."

Soon as the leaves heard the wind's loud call,
Down they came fluttering, one and all;
Over the brown fields they danced and flew,
Singing the glad little songs they knew.

"Cricket, goodbye, we've been friends so long;
Little brook, sing us your farewell song;
Say you are sorry to see us go;
Ah, you will miss us, right well we know.

"Dear little lambs in your fleecy fold,
Mother will keep you from harm and cold;
Fondly we watched you in vale and glade;
Say, will you dream of our loving shade?"

Dancing and whirling, the little leaves went;
Winter had called them, and they were content;
Soon, fast asleep in their earthy beds,
The snow laid a coverlid over their heads.

George Cooper

THE SUN

I told the Sun that I was glad,
I'm sure I don't know why;
Somehow the pleasant way he had
Of shining in the sky,
Just put a notion in my head
That wouldn't it be fun
If, walking on the hill, I said
"I'm happy" to the Sun.

John Drinkwater

LAUGHING SONG

When the green woods laugh with the voice of joy,
And the dimpling stream runs laughing by;
When the air does laugh with our merry wit,
And the green hill laughs with the noise of it;

When the meadows laugh with lively green,
And the grasshopper laughs in the merry scene;
When Mary and Susan and Emily
With their sweet round mouths sing, "Ha ha he!"

When the painted birds laugh in the shade,
When our table with cherries and nuts is spread;
Come live and be merry and join with me,
To sing the sweet chorus of "Ha ha he!"

William Blake

FROLIC

The children were shouting together
And racing along the sands,
A glimmer of dancing shadows,
A dovelike flutter of hands.

The stars were shouting in heaven,
The sun was chasing the moon:
The game was the same as the children's,
They danced to the self-same tune.

The whole of the world was merry,
One joy from the vale to the height,
Where the blue woods of twilight encircled
The lovely lawns of the light.

A. E. (G. W. Russell)

MY SHADOW

I have a little shadow that goes in and out with me,
And what can be the use of him is more than I can see.
He is very, very like me from the heels up to the head;
And I see him jump before me when I jump into my bed.

The funniest thing about him is the way he likes to grow—
Not at all like proper children, which is always very slow;
For he sometimes shoots up taller like an india-rubber ball,
And he sometimes gets so little that there's none of him at all.

He hasn't got a notion of how children ought to play,
And can only make a fool of me in every sort of way.
He stays so close beside me, he's a coward you can see;
I'd think shame to stick to nursie as that shadow sticks to me!

One morning, very early, before the sun was up,
I rose and found the shining dew on every buttercup;
But my lazy little shadow, like an arrant sleepy-head,
Had stayed at home behind me and was fast asleep in bed.

Robert Louis Stevenson

WE THANK THEE

For mothers' love and fathers' care,
For brothers strong and sisters fair,
For love at home and here each day,
For guidance lest we go astray,
Father in heaven, we thank Thee.

For flowers that bloom about our feet,
For tender grass, so fresh, so sweet,
For song of bird and hum of bee,
For all things fair we hear or see,
Father in heaven, we thank Thee.

For blue of stream and blue of sky,
For pleasant shade of branches high,
For fragrant air and cooling breeze,
For beauty of the blooming trees,
Father in heaven, we thank Thee.

Author Unknown

FUN IN A GARRET

We're having a lovely time to-day!
We're all of us up in the garret at play!
We have three houses under the eaves—
Not real, you know, but make-believes;
Two we live in, and one is a store,
Where a little old screen makes a truly door.
Warren keeps store, and Joe is his clerk,
And Betty and I stay at home and work.
Joe comes around and knocks or rings,
And we order potatoes and steaks and things;
And sometimes we go to the store and buy,
Or send the children for ribbons or pie.
It's lots of fun—just try it some day
When it rains too hard to go out and play.

Emma C. Dowd

A GOOD PLAY

We built a ship upon the stairs
All made of the back-bedroom chairs,
And filled it full of sofa pillows
To go a-sailing on the billows.

We took a saw and several nails,
And water in the nursery pails;
And Tom said, "Let us also take
An apple and a slice of cake";—
Which was enough for Tom and me
To go a-sailing on, till tea.

We sailed along for days and days,
And had the very best of plays;
But Tom fell out and hurt his knee,
So there was no one left but me.

Robert Louis Stevenson

LESSON FROM A SUN-DIAL

Ignore dull days; forget the showers;
Keep count of only shining hours.

from the German, adapted by Louis Untermeyer

Good Friends and Loyal Pals

DOORBELLS

You never know with a doorbell
Who may be ringing it—
It may be Great-aunt Cynthia
To spend the day and knit;
It may be a peddler with things to sell
(I'll buy some when I'm older),
Or the grocer's boy with his apron on
And a basket on his shoulder;
It may be the old umbrella-man
Giving his queer, cracked call,
Or a lady dressed in rustly silk,
With card-case and parasol.
Doorbells are like a magic game,
Or the grab-bag at a fair—
You never know when you hear one ring
Who may be waiting there!

Rachel Field

CROCUSES

The sunrise tints the dew;
The yellow crocuses are out,
And I must pick a few.

Josa

THE SNOWMAN

In our yard there stood a Snowman
Big and white and dignified,
But he wasn't very happy
All alone and cold, outside.

He was sure he'd feel much better
In the house where, he could see,
There were merry children playing
Just as warm as warm could be.

So he whistled to the North Wind,
"Blow me in the house, I pray,
Where it's nice and warm. I'm frozen
Standing in the snow all day."

So the North Wind roughly blew him
Right in through the cottage door,
And the Snowman now is nothing
But a puddle on the floor.

Author Unknown

THREE THINGS
TO REMEMBER

A Robin Redbreast in a cage
Puts all Heaven in a rage.

A skylark wounded on the wing
Doth make a cherub cease to sing.

He who shall hurt the little wren
Shall never be beloved by men.

William Blake

HURT NO
LIVING THING

Hurt no living thing:
Ladybird, no butterfly,
Nor moth with dusty wing,
No cricket chirping cheerily,
Nor grasshopper so light of leap,
Nor dancing gnat, no beetle fat,
Nor harmless worms that creep.

Christina Rossetti

A Bird Came Down the Walk

A Bird came down the Walk—
He did not know I saw—
He bit an Angleworm in halves
And ate the fellow, raw,

And then he drank a Dew
From a convenient Grass—
And then hopped sidewise to the Wall
To let a Beetle pass. . . .

Emily Dickinson

Little Robin Redbreast

Little Robin Redbreast sat upon a tree;
Up went Pussycat, and down went he.
Down came Pussycat, and away Robin ran;
Said little Robin Redbreast, "Catch me if you can."

Little Robin Redbreast jumped upon a wall;
Pussycat jumped after him, and almost got a fall.
Little Robin chirped and sang, and what did Pussy say?
Pussycat said naught but "Mew," and Robin flew away.

Author Unknown

Caterpillar

Brown and furry
Caterpillar in a hurry
Take your walk
To the shady leaf, or stalk,
Or what not,
Which may be the chosen spot.
No toad spy you,
Hovering bird of prey pass by you;
Spin and die,
To live again a **butterfly.**

Christina Rossetti

FRIENDS

How good to lie a little while
And look up through the tree!
The sky is like a kind, big smile
Bent sweetly over me.

The sunshine flickers through the lace
Of leaves above my head
And kisses me upon the face
Like Mother before bed.

The wind comes stealing o'er the grass
To whisper pretty things;
And though I cannot see him pass,
I feel his careful wings.

So many gentle friends are near
Whom one can scarcely see;
A child should never feel a fear
Wherever he may be.

Abbie Farwell Brown

THERE ISN'T TIME

There isn't time, there isn't time
To do the things I want to do,
With all the mountain-tops to climb,
And all the woods to wander through,
And all the seas to sail upon,
And everywhere there is to go,
And all the people, every one
Who lives upon the earth, to know.
There's only time, there's only time
To know a few, and do a few,
And then sit down and make a rhyme
About the rest I want to do.

Eleanor Farjeon

KINDNESS TO ANIMALS

Little children, never give
Pain to things that feel and live;
Let the gentle robin come
For the crumbs you save at home—
As his meat you throw along
He'll repay you with a song.
Never hurt the timid hare
Peeping from her green grass lair;
Let her come and sport and play
On the lawn at close of day.
The little lark goes soaring high
To the bright windows of the sky,
Singing as if 'twere always spring,
And fluttering on an untired wing—
Oh! let him sing his happy song,
Nor do these gentle creatures wrong.

Author Unknown

HEARTH

A cat sat quaintly by the fire
And watched the burning coals
And watched the little flames aspire
Like small decrepit souls.
Queer little fire with coals so fat
And crooked flames that rise,
No queerer than the little cat
With fire in its eyes.

Peggy Bacon

DONKEY, DONKEY

Donkey, donkey,
Old and gray,
Open your mouth
And gently bray;
Lift your ears
And blow your horn,
To wake the world
This sleepy morn.

Author Unknown

POEM

As the cat
climbed over
the top of

the jamcloset
first the right
forefoot

carefully
then the hind
stepped down

into the pit of
the empty
flower pot

William Carlos Williams

THIS HAPPY DAY

Every morning when the sun
Comes smiling up on everyone,
It's lots of fun
To say good morning to the sun.
Good morning, Sun!

Every evening after play
When the sunshine goes away,
It's nice to say,
Thank you for this happy day,
This happy Day!

Harry Behn

WHAT ROBIN TOLD

How do robins build their nests?
Robin Redbreast told me—
First a wisp of yellow hay
In a pretty round they lay;
Then some shreds of downy floss,
Feathers too and bits of moss,
Woven with a sweet, sweet song,
This way, that way, and across:
That's what Robin told me.

Where do robins hide their nests?
Robin Redbreast told me—
Up among the leaves so deep,
Where the sunbeams rarely creep,
Long before the winds are cold,
Long before the leaves are gold,
Bright-eyed stars will peep and see
Baby robins—one, two, three:
That's what Robin told me.

George Cooper

THE SECRET

We have a secret, just we three,
The Robin and I and the sweet cherry tree;
The bird told the tree and the tree told me,
And nobody knows it but just us three.

Of course Mrs. Robin knows it the best
For she built the—oh, I can't tell you the rest—
And laid the four little somethings in it—
I fear I shall say what they are any minute!

But if neither the tree nor the Robin will tell
I'm sure I can keep the sweet secret as well,
Though I know that when baby birds fly all about
The wonderful secret of spring will be out!

Author Unknown

THE LITTLE BUSY BEE

How doth the little busy bee
Improve each shining hour
And gather honey all the day
From every passing flower!

How skillfully she builds her cell;
How neat she spreads the wax!
And labours hard to store it well
With the sweet food she makes.

Isaac Watts

Holidays and Happy

Days

SPRINKLING

Sometimes in the summer
When the day is hot
Daddy takes the garden hose
And finds a shady spot;
Then he calls me over,
Looks at my bare toes
And says, "Why, you need sprinkling,
You thirsty little rose!"

Dorothy Mason Pierce

SUMMER VACATION

School is over,
Oh, what fun!
Lessons finished,
Play begun.
Who'll run fastest,
You or I?
Who'll laugh loudest?
Let us try.

Kate Greenaway

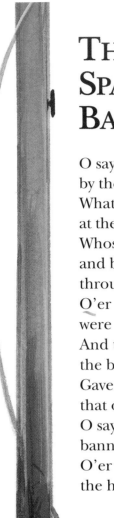

THE STAR-SPANGLED BANNER

O say, can you see,
by the dawn's early light,
What so proudly we hailed
at the twilight's last gleaming?
Whose broad stripes
and bright stars,
through the perilous fight,
O'er the ramparts we watched
were so gallantly streaming!
And the rockets' red glare,
the bombs bursting in air,
Gave proof through the night
that our flag was still there:
O say, does that star-spangled
banner yet wave
O'er the land of the free and
the home of the brave?

Francis Scott Key

THE FLAG GOES BY

Hats off!
Along the street there comes
A blare of bugles, a ruffle of drums,
A flash of color beneath the sky:
Hats off!
The flag is passing by!

Blue and crimson and white it shines,
Over the steel-tipped, ordered lines.
Hats off!
The colors before us fly;
But more than the flag is passing by.

Sea-fights and land-fights, grim and great,
Fought to make and to save the State:
Weary marches and sinking ships;
Cheers of victory on dying lips;

Days of plenty and years of peace;
March of a strong land's swift increase;
Equal justice, right, and law,
Stately honor and reverend awe;

Sign of a nation, great and strong,
To ward her people from foreign wrong:

I HEAR AMERICA SINGING

I hear America singing, the varied carols I hear,
Those of the mechanics, each singing his as it should be
     blithe and strong,
The carpenter singing his as he measures his plank or beam,
The mason singing his as he makes ready for work or
     leaves off work,
The boatman singing what belongs to him in his boat, the
     deck hand singing on the steamboat deck,
The shoemaker singing as he sits on his bench, the hatter
     singing as he stands,
The wood-cutter's song, the ploughboy's on his way in the
     morning, or at noon intermission or at sundown,
The delicious singing of the mother, or the young wife at
     work, or the girl sewing or washing,
Each sings what belongs to him or her and to none else,
The day what belongs to the day—at night the party of
     young fellows, robust, friendly,
Singing with open mouths their strong melodious songs.

Walt Whitman

Pride and glory and honor—all
Live in the colors to stand or fall.

Hats off!
Along the street there comes
A blare of bugles, a ruffle of drums;
And loyal hearts are beating high:
Hats off!
The flag is passing by!

Henry Holcomb Bennett

THEME IN YELLOW

I spot the hills
With yellow balls in autumn.
I light the prairie cornfields
Orange and tawny gold clusters
And I am called pumpkins.
On the last of October
When dusk is fallen
Children join hands
And circle round me
Singing ghost songs
And love to the harvest moon;
I am a jack-o'-lantern
With terrible teeth
And the children know
I am fooling.

Carl Sandburg

HALLOWE'EN

Tonight is the night
When dead leaves fly
Like witches on switches
Across the sky,
When elf and sprite
Flit through the night
On a moony sheen.

Tonight is the night
When leaves make a sound
Like a gnome in his home
Under the ground,
When spooks and trolls
Creep out of holes
Mossy and green.

Tonight is the night
When pumpkins stare
Through sheaves and leaves
Everywhere,
When ghoul and ghost
And goblin host
Dance round their queen.
It's Hallowe'en!

Harry Behn

THE FIRST THANKSGIVING OF ALL

Peace and Mercy and Jonathan,
And Patience (very small),
Stood by the table giving thanks
The first Thanksgiving of all.
There was very little for them to eat,
Nothing special and nothing sweet;
Only bread and a little broth,
And a bit of fruit (and no tablecloth);
But Peace and Mercy and Jonathan
And Patience in a row,
Stood up and asked a blessing on
Thanksgiving, long ago.

Thankful they were their ship had come
Safely across the sea;
Thankful they were for hearth and home,
And kin and company;
They were glad of broth to go with their bread,
Glad their apples were round and red,
Glad of mayflowers they would bring
Out of the woods again next spring.

Nancy Byrd Turner

THE PILGRIM

Who would true valour see,
Let him come hither!
One here will constant be,
Come wind, come weather;
There's no discouragement
Shall make him once relent
His firm-avowed intent
    To be a Pilgrim.

Whoso beset him round
With dismal stories,
Do but themselves confound;
His strength the more is.
No lion can him fright;
He'll with a giant fight;
But he will have a right
    To be a Pilgrim.

Nor enemy, nor friend,
Can daunt his spirit;
He knows he at the end
Shall Life inherit:—
Then, fancies, fly away;
He'll not fear what men say:
He'll labour, night and day,
    To be a Pilgrim.

John Bunyan

WE THANK THEE

For flowers so beautiful and sweet,
For friends and clothes and food to eat,
For precious hours, for work and play,
We thank Thee this Thanksgiving Day.

For Father's care and Mother's love,
For the blue sky and clouds above,
For springtime and autumn gay
We thank Thee this Thanksgiving Day.

For all Thy gifts so good and fair,
Bestowed so freely everywhere,
Give us grateful hearts we pray,
To thank Thee this Thanksgiving Day.

Mattie M. Renwick

THE PILGRIMS CAME

The Pilgrims came across the sea
And never thought of you and me;
And yet it's very strange the way
We think of them Thanksgiving Day.

We tell their story, old and true,
Of how they sailed across the blue
And found a new land to be free
And built their homes quite near the sea.

Every child knows well the tale
Of how they bravely turned the sail
And journeyed many a day and night
To worship God as they thought right.

The people think that they were sad
And grave; I'm sure that they were glad.
They made Thanksgiving Day that's fun.
We thank the Pilgrims, every one.

Annette Wynne

THE CHRISTMAS SILENCE

Hushed are the pigeons cooing low
On dusty rafters of the loft;
And mild-eyed oxen, breathing soft,
Sleep on the fragrant hay below.

Dim shadows in the corner hide;
The glimmering lantern's rays are shed
Where one young lamb just lifts his head,
Then huddles 'gainst his mother's side.

Strange silence tingles in the air;
Through the half-open door a bar
Of light from one low-hanging star
Touches a baby's radiant hair.

No sound—the mother, kneeling, lays
Her cheek against the little face.
Oh human love! Oh heavenly grace!
'Tis yet in silence that she prays.

Ages of silence end tonight;
Then to the long-expectant earth
Glad angels come to greet His birth
In burst of music, love, and light!

Margaret Deland

A CHRISTMAS FOLK SONG

The little Jesus came to town;
The wind blew up, the wind blew down;
Out in the street the wind was bold;
Now who would house Him from the cold?

Then opened wide a stable door,
Fair were the rushes on the floor;
The Ox put forth a horned head:
"Come, little Lord, here make Thy bed."

Up rose the Sheep were folded near:
"Thou Lamb of God, come, enter here."
He entered there to rush and reed,
Who was the Lamb of God indeed.

The little Jesus came to town;
With ox and sheep He laid Him down;
Peace to the byre, peace to the fold,
For that they housed Him from the cold!

Lizette Woodworth Reese

JESUS, OUR BROTHER

Jesus our brother, kind and good,
Was humbly born in a stable rude;
The friendly beasts around Him stood,
Jesus our brother, kind and good.

"I," said the **donkey,** shaggy and brown,
"I carried His mother up hill and down;
I carried her safely to Bethlehem town,
I," said the **donkey,** shaggy and brown.

"I," said the **cow,** all white and red,
"I gave Him my manger for His bed;
I gave Him my hay to pillow His head,
I," said the **cow,** all white and red.

"I," said the **sheep** with the curly horn,
"I gave Him my wool for a blanket warm.
He wore my coat on Christmas morn,
I," said the **sheep** with the curly horn.

"I," said the **dove** from the rafters high,
"I cooed Him to sleep so He would not cry,
I cooed Him to sleep, my mate and I,
I," said the **dove** from the rafters high.

And every beast, by some good spell,
In the stable dark was glad to tell,
Of the gift he gave Immanuel,
The gift he gave Immanuel.

Author Unknown

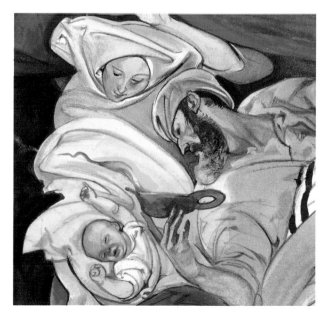

LONG, LONG AGO

Winds through the olive trees
Softly did blow,
Round little Bethlehem
Long, long ago.

Sheep on the hillside lay
Whiter than snow;
Shepherds were watching them,
Long, long ago.

Then from the happy sky,
Angels bent low,
Singing their songs of joy,
Long, long ago.

For in a manger bed,
Cradled we know,
Christ came to Bethlehem,
Long, long ago.

Author Unknown

THE SHEPHERD
AND THE KING

The Shepherd and the King,
The Angel and the Ass,
They heard Sweet Mary sing
When her joy was come to pass;
They heard Sweet Mary sing
To the Baby on her knee;
Sing again, Sweet Mary,
And we will sing with thee!

Earth, bear a berry!
Heaven, bear a light!
Man, make you merry
On Christmas Night.

Eleanor Farjeon

CHRISTMAS CAROL

The Christ-child lay on Mary's lap,
His hair was like a light.
(O weary, weary was the world,
But here is all aright.)

The Christ-child lay on Mary's breast,
His hair was like a star.
(O stern and cunning are the kings,
But here the true hearts are.)

The Christ-child lay on Mary's heart,
His hair was like a fire.
(O weary, weary is the world,
But here the world's desire.)

The Christ-child stood at Mary's knee,
His hair was like a crown,
And all the flowers looked up at Him
And all the stars looked down.

Gilbert K. Chesterton

MY GIFT

What can I give Him
Poor as I am;
If I were a shepherd,
I would give Him a lamb.
If I were a wise man,
I would do my part.
But what can I give Him?
I will give my heart.

Christina Rossetti

BELLS OF CHRISTMAS

Why do bells of Christmas ring?
Why do little children sing?

Once a lovely shining star,
Seen by shepherds from afar,
Gently moved until its light
Made a manger's cradle bright.

There a darling baby lay
Pillowed soft upon the hay;
And its mother sang and smiled:
"This is Christ, the holy Child!"

Therefore bells for Christmas ring,

Therefore little children sing.

Eugene Field

Index of Authors

A

A. E. (G. W. Russell), *Frolic* 54
Abbey, Henry, *What Do We Plant?* 16
Aldis, Dorothy, *Feet* 9
Aldis, Dorothy, *I Never Hear* 41
Asch, Frank, *Puddles* 49
Author Unknown, *We Thank Thee* 56
Author Unknown, *Childhood* 50
Author Unknown, *Cradle Song* 41
Author Unknown, *Doctor Foster* 14
Author Unknown, *One Misty, Moisty Morning* 14
Author Unknown, *When Mother Reads Aloud* 23
Author Unknown, *Mr. Nobody* 33
Author Unknown, *Evening Song* 42
Author Unknown, *To the Wayfarer* 16
Author Unknown, *The Snowman* 60
Author Unknown, *Little Robin Redbreast* 62
Author Unknown, *Kindness to Animals* 66
Author Unknown, *Donkey, Donkey* 66
Author Uknown, *The Secret* 68
Author Unknown, *Jesus, Our Brother* 81
Author Unknown, *Long, Long Ago* 82

B

Bacon, Peggy, *Hearth* 66
Behn, Harry, *Hallowe'en* 75
Behn, Harry, *Spring Rain* 14
Behn, Harry, *This Happy Day* 67
Bennett, Henry Holcomb, *The Flag Goes By* 72
Blake, William, *Laughing Song* 53
Blake, William, *Three Things to Remember* 61
Brown, Abbie Farwell, *Friends* 65
Brown, Thomas Edward, *My Garden* 39
Bunyan, John, *The Pilgrim* 76
Butts, Mary F., *Winter Night* 40

C

Carney, Julia Fletcher, *Little Things* 39
Chesterton, G. K. *Christmas Carol* 83
Coatsworth, Elizabeth, *Swift Things Are Beautiful* 51
Conkling, Hilda, *Water* 14
Cooper, George, *Come, Little Leaves* 52
Cooper, George, *Only One Mother* 41
Cooper, George, *What Robin Told* 68
Crosby, Ernest, *In the Garden* 38

D

Davies, Mary Carolyn, *Be Different to Trees* 13
de la Mare, Walter, *The Little Green Orchard* 29
Deland, Margaret, *The Christmas Silence* 78
Dickinson, Emily, *A Book* 20
Dickinson, Emily, *A Bird Came Down the Walk* 62
Dodge, Mary Mapes, *Snowflakes* 18
Dowd, Emma C., *Fun in a Garret* 57

Drinkwater, John, *The Sun* 53
Driscoll, Louise, *Hold Fast Your Dreams* 26

E-G

E-Yeh-Shure, *Beauty* 49
Farjeon, Eleanor, *The Shepherd and the King* 83
Farjeon, Eleanor, *There Isn't Time* 65
Field, Eugene, *Bells of Christmas* 84
Field, Rachel, *Doorbells* 58
Follen, Eliza Lee, *The Moon* 44
Greenaway, Kate, *Summer Vacation* 71
Guiterman, Arthur, *House Blessing* 39
Guiterman, Arthur, *Of Courtesy* 35

H

Huff, Barbara A., *The Library* 30
Hughes, Langston, *In Time of Silver Rain* 14
Hughes, Langston, *April Rain Song* 49
Hughes, Langston, *Dreams* 22
Hugo, Victor, *Be Like the Bird* 23
Hugo, Victor, *Good Night* 36

J-L

Jackson, Leroy F., *I've Got a New Book from My Grandfather Hyde* 33
Josa, *Crocuses* 57
Key, Francis Scott, *The Star-Spangled Banner* 72
Lang, Andrew, *I'd Leave* 31
Loveman, Robert, *April Rain* 15
Lowell, Amy *Sea Shell* 11

M-P

Millay, Edna St. Vincent, *Afternoon on a Hill* 50
Milne, A. A., *Knight-in-Armour* 20
Milne, A. A., *Politeness* 35
Mitchell, Lucy Sprague, *It Is Raining* 24
Morley, Christopher, *Animal Crackers* 42
Nesbit, Wilbur D., *Who Hath a Book* 32
Pierce, Dorothy Mason, *Good Night* 36
Pierce, Dorothy Mason, *Sprinkling* 71

R

Rands,William Brighty, *The World* 10
Reese, Lizette Woodworth, *A Christmas Folk Song* 79
Renwick, Mattie M., *We Thank Thee* 77
Rossetti, Christina, *Caterpillar* 63
Rossetti, Christina, *Hurt no Living Thing* 61
Rossetti, Christina, *My Gift* 84
Rossetti, Christina, *Who Has Seen the Wind?* 19

S

Sandburg, Carl, *Theme in Yellow* 75
Shakespeare, William, *A Violet Bank* 13
Snyder, Zilpha Keatley, *To Dark Eyes Dreaming* 26
Stevenson, Robert Louis, *The Land of Story-Books* 33
Stevenson, Robert Louis, *Whole Duty of Children* 35
Stevenson, Robert Louis, *The Wind* 19
Stevenson, Robert Louis, *The Moon* 44
Stevenson, Robert Louis, *Good and Bad Children* 46
Stevenson, Robert Louis, *The Swing* 47

Stevenson, Robert Louis, *My Shadow* 54
Stevenson, Robert Louis, *A Good Play* 57
Stuart, Jesse, *My Land Is Fair for Any Eyes to See* 13

T–V

Turner, Nancy Byrd, *The First Thanksgiving of All* 76
Untermeyer, Louis, *Lesson from a Sun-Dial* 57
Viorst, Judith, *Learning* 35
Viorst, Judith, *I Wouldn't Be Afraid* 20

W

Watts, Isaac, *The Little Busy Bee* 68
Wesley, Charles, *Evening Hymn* 36
Weston, Rebecca J., *Morning Song* 42
Whitman, Walt, *I Hear America Singing* 73
Williams, William Carlos, *Poem* 66
Wylie, Elinor, *Velvet Shoes* 19
Wynne, Annette, *The Pilgrims Came* 77

Index of Titles

A

Afternoon on a Hill 50
Animal Crackers 42
April Rain 15
April Rain Song 49

B

Beauty 49
Be Different to Trees 13
Be Like the Bird 23
Bells of Christmas 84
Bird Came Down the Walk, A 62
Book, A 20

C

Caterpillar 62
Childhood 50
Christmas Carol 83
Christmas Folk Song, A 79
Christmas Silence, The 78
Come, Little Leaves 52
Cradle Song 41
Crocuses 57

D–E

Doctor Foster 14
Donkey, Donkey 66
Doorbells 58
Dreams 22
Evening Hymn 36
Evening Song 42

F–G

Feet 9
First Thanksgiving of All, The 76
Flag Goes By, The 72
Friends 65
Frolic 54
Fun in a Garret 57
Good and Bad Children 46
Good Night 36
Good Night 36
Good Play, A 57

H

Hallowe'en 75
Hearth 66
Hold Fast Your Dreams 26
House Blessing 39
Hurt No Living Thing 61

I

I Hear America Singing 73
I Never Hear 41
I Wouldn't Be Afraid 20
I'd Leave 31
In the Garden 38
In Time of Silver Rain 14
It Is Raining 24
I've Got a New Book from
     Grandfather Hyde 33

J–K

Jesus, Our Brother 81

Kindness to Animals 66
Knight-in-Armour 20

L

Land of Story-Books, The 33
Laughing Song 53
Learning 35
Lesson from a Sun-Dial 57
Library, The 30
Little Busy Bee, The 68
Little Green Orchard, The 29
Little Robin Redbreast 62
Little Things 39
Long, Long Ago 82

M

Moon, The 44
Moon, The 44
Morning Song 42
Mr. Nobody 33
My Garden 39
My Gift 84
My Land Is Fair for Any Eyes to See 13
My Shadow 54

O

Of Courtesy 35
One Misty, Moisty Morning 14
Only One Mother 41

P

Pilgrim, The 76

Pilgrims Came, The 77
Poem 66
Politeness 35
Puddles 49

S

Sea Shell 11
Secret, The 68
Shepherd and the King, The 83
Snowflakes 18
Snowman, The 60
Spring Rain 14
Sprinkling 71
Star-Spangled Banner, The 72

Summer Vacation 71
Sun, The 53
Swift Things Are Beautiful 51
Swing, The 47

T–V

Theme in Yellow 75
There Isn't Time 65
This Happy Day 67
Three Things to Remember 61
To the Wayfarer 16
To Dark Eyes Dreaming 26
Velvet Shoes 19
Violet Bank, A 13

W

Water 14
We Thank Thee 56
We Thank Thee 77
What Do We Plant? 16
What Robin Told 68
When Mother Reads Aloud 23
Who Has Seen the Wind? 19
Who Has Seen the Wind 19
Who Hath a Book 32
Whole Duty of Children 35
Wind, The 19
Winter Night 40
World, The 10

ACKNOWLEDGMENTS (continued from page 4)

BACON, PEGGY. "Hearth" from *ANIMOSITIES*, copyright 1931, renewed 1959 by Peggy Bacon. Reprinted by permission of Harcourt Brace & Company. BEHN, HARRY. "Spring Rain," "Hallowe'en," and "This Happy Day" from *THE LITTLE HILL Poems and Pictures* by Harry Behn. Copyright 1949 by Harry Behn, © renewed 1977 by Alice L. Behn. Used by permission of Marian Reiner. CHESTERTON, G.K. "A Christmas Carol." Copyright © by A.P. Watt Limited. Reprinted by permission of A.P. Watt Limited. COATSWORTH, ELIZABETH. "Swift Things Are Beautiful." Reprinted with the permission of Simon & Schuster Books for Young Readers, an imprint of Simon & Schuster Children's Publishing Division from *AWAY GOES SALLY* by Elizabeth Coatsworth. Copyright 1934 Macmillan Publishing Company; copyright renewed © 1962 Elizabeth Coatsworth Beston. COATSWORTH, ELIZABETH. "He Who Has Never Known Hunger." Reprinted with the permission of Simon & Schuster Books for Young Readers, an imprint of Simon & Schuster Children's Publishing Division from *THE FAIR AMERICAN* by Elizabeth Coatsworth. Copyright 1940 Macmillan Publishing Company; copyright renewed © 1968 Elizabeth Coatsworth Beston. DICKINSON, EMILY. "A bird came down the walk." Reprinted by permission of the publishers and the Trustees of Amherst College from *THE POEMS OF EMILY DICKINSON*, Thomas H. Johnson, ed., Cambridge, Mass.: The Belknap Press of Harvard University Press, copyright © 1951, 1955, 1979, 1983 by the President and Fellows of Harvard College. E-YEH-SHURE. "Beauty" from *I AM A PUEBLO INDIAN GIRL*, copyright 1939 by William Morrow and Company Inc., copyright renewed 1967 by Louise Abeita Chiwiwi. Reprinted by permission of William Morrow and Company Inc. FARJEON, ELEANOR. "There Isn't Time" and "The Shepherd and the King" from *POEMS FOR CHILDREN* copyright 1933, 1951 by Eleanor Farjeon. Reprinted by permission of Harold Ober Associates Incorporated. FIELD, RACHEL. "Doorbells" reprinted by permission of Radcliffe College. GUITERMAN, ARTHUR. "House Blessing" from *DEATH AND GENERAL PUTNAM AND 101 OTHER POEMS* reprinted by permission of Louise H. Sclove. GUITERMAN, ARTHUR. "Of Courtesy" from *A POET'S PROVERBS* reprinted by permission of Louise H. Sclove. HUFF, BARBARA A. "The Library" reprinted by permission of the author. HUGHES, LANGSTON. "April Rain Song," "Dreams," and "In Time of Silver Rain" from *COLLECTED POEMS* by Langston Hughes. Copyright © 1994 by the Estate of Langston Hughes. Reprinted by permission of Alfred A. Knopf Inc. LOVEMAN, ROBERT. "April Rain" from *SUNG UNDER THE SILVER UMBRELLA* (p. 151). Reprinted by permission of the Association for Childhood Education International, 17904 Georgia Avenue, Suite 215, Olney, MD. Copyright © 1962 by the Association. MILNE, A. A. "Politeness" from *WHEN WE WERE VERY YOUNG* by A. A. Milne, illustrations by E. H. Shepard. Copyright 1924 by E.P. Dutton, renewed 1952 by A. A. Milne. Used by permission of Dutton Children's Books, a division of Penguin Putnam Inc. MILNE, A. A. "Knight-in-Armour" from *NOW WE ARE SIX* by A. A. Milne, illustrations by E. H. Shepard. Copyright 1927 by E.P. Dutton, renewed © 1955 by A. A. Milne. Used by permission of Dutton Children's Books, a division of Penguin Putnam Inc. MITCHELL, LUCY SPRAGUE. "It is Raining" from *ANOTHER HERE AND NOW STORY BOOK* by Lucy Sprague Mitchell. Copyright 1937 by E.P. Dutton, renewed © 1965 by Lucy Sprague Mitchell. Used by permission of Dutton Children's Books, a division of Penguin Putnam Inc. PIERCE, DOROTHY MASON. "Good Night" from the *THE SUSIANNA WINKLE BOOK* by Dorothy Mason Pierce. Copyright 1935 by E.P. Dutton, renewed © 1963 by Dorothy Mason Pierce. Used by permission of Dutton, a division of Penguin Putnam Inc. PIERCE, DOROTHY MASON. "Sprinkling" from *SUNG UNDER THE SILVER UMBRELLA* (p. 40). Reprinted by permission of the Association for Childhood Education International, 17904 Georgia Avenue, Suite 215, Olney, MD. Copyright © 1962 by the Association. REESE, LIZETTE WOODWORTH. "A Christmas Folksong" from *SUNG UNDER THE SILVER UMBRELLA* (p. 172). Reprinted by permission of the Association For Childhood Education International, 17904 Georgia Avenue, Suite 215, Olney, MD. Copyright © 1962 by the Association. SNYDER, ZILPHA KEATLEY. "To Dark Eyes Dreaming" from *TODAY IS SATURDAY*, copyright 1969 by Zilpha Keatley Snyder. Reprinted by permission of the author. STUART, JESSE. "My Land is Fair for Any Eyes to See" from *MAN WITH A BULL-TONGUE PLOUGH* by Jesse Stuart. Reprinted by permission of the author. TURNER, NANCY BYRD. "The First Thanksgiving of All." Reprinted by permission of Beverley T. Thomas. UNTERMEYER, LOUIS. "Lesson from a Sun-Dial" from *RAINBOW IN THE SKY* translated from the German by Louis Untermeyer, book copyright 1935 by Harcourt Brace and Company, and renewed 1963 by Louis Untermeyer, reprinted by permission of the publisher. VIORST, JUDITH. "Learning" and "I Wouldn't Be Afraid" reprinted with the permission of Atheneum Books for Young Readers, an imprint of Simon & Schuster Children's Publishing Division from *IF I WERE IN CHARGE OF THE WORLD AND OTHER WORRIES* by Judith Viorst. Copyright © 1981 by Judith Viorst. WILLIAM, WILLIAM CARLOS. "Poem" from *COLLECTED POEMS: 1909-1939 VOLUME 1*. Copyright 1938 by New Directions Publishing Corporation. Reprinted by permission of New Directions Publishing Corporation. Our sincere thanks to the following authors, whom we were unable to locate: Dorothy Aldis for "I Never Hear," Abbie Farwell Brown for "Friends," and Mattie M. Renwick for "We Thank Thee."

All possible care has been taken to fully acknowledge the ownership and use of every selection in this book. If any mistakes or omissions have occurred inadvertently, they will be corrected in subsequent editions, provided notification is sent to the publisher. Many of the poems included are traditional, with the author unknown.